Talking in the Dark

Talking

in the

Dark

poems by

WESLEY MCNAIR

David R. Godine, Publisher
Boston

First published in 1998 by
David R. Godine, Publisher, Inc.
Box 450
Jaffrey, New Hampshire 03452

Library of Congress Cataloging-in-Publication Data

McNair, Wesley.
    Talking in the dark : poems / by Wesley McNair.
        p.   cm.
    I. Title.
    PS3563.C388T35   1998
    811'.54--DC21   98-33665
                        CIP

ISBN: 1-56792-094-2

First edition, 1998

This book was printed on acid-free paper

Printed in the United States of America

For my children: David, Joel, Sean, and Shanna

Acknowledgments

Grateful acknowledgment is made to the following magazines in which poems in this collection have previously appeared:

TheBlueMoon (online): "Disavowal";
The Boston Review: "First Class in Night School";
Gettysburg Review: "History by George B. Yeaton";
Green Mountains Review: "Old Cadillacs";
Michigan Quarterly Review: "The Weight";
Mid-American Review: "The Characters of Dirty Jokes";
New England Review: "Love Handles," "Poem for My Feet";
New Virginia Review: "Faces," "Shaking Hands";
Ohio Review: "Old Talk" (part 4);
Poetry International: "The Book of A";
Poetry Northwest: "The Lover," "The Match," "Old Guys," "The Puppy,"
    "Waving Goodbye," "Why We Need Poetry";
Potato Eyes: "Big Dog, Little Dog";
The Portsmouth Review: "The Last Trick";
The Sewanee Review: "Fine," "Losses," "Speaking of Time";
Sport Literate: "The Retarded Children Play Baseball";
Victory Park: "As They Are";
Witness: "Weeds";
Yankee: "Glass Night."

"Trying to Find Her Teeth" originally appeared in *Poetry.* Copyright
    © 1990 by the Modern Poetry Association.

"Blame," "The Cabbie," and "The Wish" are reprinted from *Prairie
    Schooner* by permission of the University of Nebraska Press.
    Copyright © 1998 by the University of Nebraska Press.

"Glass Night" was reprinted by *Yankee* as winner of first prize for best
    poem published in the magazine during 1994.

"The Characters of Dirty Jokes" is for Anne; "The Future" and "Love Handles" are for Diane.

Special thanks to Diane McNair, Donald Hall, David Scribner, Jean Scribner, Robert Kimber, and Patricia O'Donnell.

Contents

FINE

LOVE HANDLES

Old Guys

THE LOVER

He is such an unlikely lover, wearing sneakers
someone has dressed him in, his old
floppy legs hanging down from the bed
they have sold his house for. What he loves
is not even here, and when he rocks
this way, his head thrown back, holding only himself,
he is not much more than a chest
heaving and a few teeth you can almost
see right through. It is the clear refusal
to open his eyes and be where he is
among the pleading nurses and his roommate,
the sad, lost man, that sets him apart.
It is how he will not let go
of all he does not have, making up this song
about it, this love song, which fills
the lonely hall outside his room and no one can stop.

OLD TALK

1

Speaking of her wealthy sister-in-law,
the old woman doubles the only
fist she has: "This is how
she used to hit him," she says, tapping
her knuckles on her flaccid arm.
"Got him so he'd put his head in her lap
the minute he did anything wrong
so she could spank him."
She has forgotten the cane
across her lap, the pill bottles beside her
on the stand, her remote for the TV.
"She don't have to put on airs with me,"
she says, still making the fist,
ready at last for the fight
that has been coming for sixty years.

2

She was always correcting
her husband in front of company,
so when she accused him
of leaving the most important
part out of his story,
and he smiled, waving her away
like smoke from his pipe,
we couldn't help but be pleased

by the change in him.
Later, in the nursing home,
when he'd forgotten even this
story, we saw what all
that time she had needed
to tell others, though now
when she corrected him
for eating his dessert before
his soup, the others —
she sought with her eyes
weren't much different
from him, and he turned away
from her in his chair,
needing only to be left alone
with his sweet cookie.

3

After their long marriage, Red's wife
died of cancer, and now his peter's dead.
He can't understand why, he says,
and his hairdresser girlfriend doesn't get it,
either. That woman is after him
all the time, he says, and he's tired of how
she complains about his poodle, the one
with the same name he gave the poodle
he and his wife owned for years. Oh,
she's a real lover, Red says, in the chair
with the dog, who climbs all over
him and licks his lips as if she were.

4

The old man who lives by himself wants me to know
he has a gun and the military document that proves
he understands how to use it, though when he brings in
the pleated envelope that looks like a purse
to search for his discharge from the army,
all he can find is this yellow, hand-drawn
valentine from his wife's dog, which he opens,
then shakes his head at its message and carefully
hands to me: "Ma says to tell you she loves you."

OLD GUYS

Driving beyond a turn in the mist
of a certain morning, you'll find them
beside a men-at-work sign,
standing around with their caps on
like penguins, all bellies and bills.
They'll be watching what the yellow truck
is doing and how. Old guys know trucks,
having spent days on their backs under them
or cars. You've seen the gray face
of the garage mechanic lying on his pallet, old
before his time, and the gray, as he turns
his wrench looking up through the smoke
of his cigarette, around the pupil
of his eye. This comes from concentrating
on things the rest of us refuse
to be bothered with, like the thickening
line of dirt in front of the janitor's
push broom as he goes down the hall, or the same
ten eyelets inspector number four checks
on the shoe, or the box after box
the newspaper man brings to a stop
in the morning dark outside the window
of his car. Becoming expert in such details
is what has made the retired old guy
behind the shopping cart at the discount store
appear so lost. Beside him his large wife,
who's come through poverty and starvation
of feeling, hungry for promises of more
for less, knows just where she is,

and where and who she is sitting by his side
a year or so later in the hospital
as he lies stunned by the failure of his heart
or lung. "Your father" is what she calls him,
wearing her permanent expression
of sadness, and the daughter, obese
and starved herself, calls him "Daddy,"
a child's word, crying for a tenderness
the two of them never knew. Nearby, her husband,
who resembles his father-in-law in spite
of his Elvis sideburns, doesn't say
even to himself what's going on inside him,
only grunts and stares as if the conversation
they were having concerned a missing bolt
or some extra job the higher-ups just gave him
because this is what you do when you're bound,
after an interminable, short life, to be an old guy.

HISTORY BY GEORGE B. YEATON

*Notes left by George B. Yeaton for a town history
of Epsom, New Hampshire*

Once, above the fading and
blotted loops of his antique
calligraphy,

the man who wrote it sat entering
the date and signing his name, George B.
Yeaton, relieved

to have written these words in time:
"With the death of Ernest M. Green
last Thursday

August 30 there are only three men left
from the crew that worked with me at the mill
in 1905." Which mill,

we cannot ask George B., now vanished
from the crew himself, nor ask the names
of the men

he somehow chose to designate in another
note as Mr. L., Mr. B., and Mr. W.,
some of whom

would not speak to each other
one afternoon on a farm
somewhere

while threshing, but who had a conversation
anyway: "Mr. L. talked to Mr. W., Mr. W.
talked to me,

Mr. W. talked to Mr. L., Mr. B. talked
to me, I talked to all three. George
B. Yeaton."

What can the patient reader
do, not even having a motive
for why,

in still another entry, the poor first-
nameless wife of Daniel W. Pierce
hanged herself

from one of the largest
apple trees "in her husband's
orchard"—

what, but think of history
as the facts that are arranged
and lost

by one whose reasons for telling it
aren't always clear? Yet clarity
might obscure

George B.'s unwitting point about the lack of it
in history, whether or not the version's
contained in loopy notes

like those of his long, dateless story
recalled from childhood about Aunts Nabby
and Molly singing

in the darkness on a sleigh ride, ignoring
the widely known adage that it was dreadful
to sing outdoors

at night and frightening him to tears.
"I will never forget that music," he wrote,
and signed his name

and took the memory of which song it was
along with the world that believed in this
odd adage

with him, where most of what we love
or fear or vow always to remember
finally goes,

mysterious in spite of us, beyond the power
of history, George Yeaton's or anyone's,
to sum up or explain.

OLD CADILLACS

Who would have guessed they would end this way,
rubbing shoulders with old Scouts and pickups
at the laundromat, smoothing out frost heaves

all the way home? Once cherished for their style,
they are now valued for use, their back seats
full of kids, dogs steaming their windows; yet this

is the life they have wanted all along, to let go
of their flawless paint jobs and carry cargoes
of laundry and cheap groceries down no-name roads,

wearing bumper stickers that promise Christ
until they can travel no more and take their places
in backyards, far from the heated garages

of the rich who rejected them, among old tires
and appliances and chicken wire, where the poor
keep each one, dreaming, perhaps, of a Cadillac

with parts so perfect it might lift past sixty
as if not touching the earth at all, as if to pass
through the eye of a needle and roll into heaven.

AS THEY ARE

Maybe because the post office lady has a post office
made out of a house, she built a house that looks like
a post office. You can't say for sure why any
of the houses here look this way, though some seem
to offer their own explanations: We weren't able
to fix all of it, for instance, is common, or Later,
we changed our minds, or the comprehensive Yes
but it works, which includes both of the others,
and accounts for the cape half wrapped in plastic
against the cold of this winter day, and the four-pane
window on a slant letting in the light between
the porch roof and the eaves. What the houses might
have been or ought to look like drifts like smoke
from their chimneys up into some other world.
Here in their world they remain just as they are.

THE FUTURE

On the afternoon talk shows of America
the guests have suffered life's sorrows
long enough. All they require now
is the opportunity for closure,
to put the whole thing behind them
and get on with their lives. That their lives,
in fact, are getting on with them even
as they announce their requirement
is written on the faces of the younger ones
wrinkling their brows, and the skin
of their elders collecting just under their
set chins. It's not easy to escape the past,
but who wouldn't want to live in a future
where the worst has already happened
and Americans can finally relax after daring
to demand a different way? For the rest of us,
the future, barring variations, turns out
to be not so different from the present
where we have always lived—the same
struggle of wishes and losses, and hope,
that old lieutenant, picking us up
every so often to dust us off and adjust
our helmets. Adjustment, for that matter,
may be the one lesson hope has to give,
serving us best when we begin to find
what we didn't know we wanted in what
the future brings. Nobody would have asked
for the ice storm that takes down trees
and knocks the power out, leaving nothing

but two buckets of snow melting
on the wood stove and candlelight so weak,
the old man sitting at the kitchen table
can hardly see to play cards. Yet how else
but by the old woman's laughter
when he mistakes a jack for a queen
would he look at her face in the half-light as if
for the first time while the kitchen around them
and the very cards he holds in his hands
disappear? In the deep moment of his looking
and her looking back, there is no future,
only right now, all, anyway, each one of us
has ever had, and all the two of them,
sitting together in the dark among the cracked
notes of the snow thawing beside them
on the stove, right now will ever need.

The Book of A

THE PUPPY

From down the road, starting up
and stopping once more, the sound
of a puppy on a chain who has not yet
discovered he will spend his life there.
Foolish dog, to forget where he is
and wander until he feels the collar
close fast around his throat, then cry
all over again about the little space
in which he finds himself. Soon,
when there is no grass left in it
and he understands it is all he has,
he will snarl and bark whenever
he senses a threat to it.
Who would believe this small
sorrow could lead to such fury
no one would ever come near him?

FIRST CLASS IN NIGHT SCHOOL

Among anxious housewives taking notes
and searching for the correct page,
he is the one who speaks,
explaining in his deep, full voice
that the question puts him in mind
of the very thing he was asked to consider
in a previous class, and in fact of a particular
term which, suddenly, he cannot recall
though he tries, starting his whole sentence
again, until all he can think to do
is make a small hole between his lips
and whistle the sound of uh-oh,
uh-oh into this silence, the one which he—
like the others now turning to look at his big
ears and the upturned mouth that goes right on
with its odd chirping—has most feared.

THE CABBIE

Up front in the dark he is nothing
but a back and the back
of a head, but then he brings
the sights of the city at night
to my window, filling the cab
with his jokes, so by the time
he takes the photograph
of his girlfriend down from its place
on the visor above him, flicking
on the dome light, I'm all
smiles too. She's the one
who keeps me in the cab every night,
especially with the marriage
coming up, he says, smiling back
in the rearview mirror with part
of his face. But now I'm not sure
the woman in the photo, which looks
shiny and has scissored edges,
is his girlfriend at all,
and leaning forward to hand it
back to him, I notice how fat
he is, his stomach pressed up
against the steering wheel,
understanding at last, the light
off again, this is his world:
two soft chairs on moaning tires,
and him, and me, the visitor
who sits with him, laughing as others

have laughed, and talking,
and watching the city shine around us
as he drives through the dark.

THE WEIGHT

Of course, the ones
who came to his office
might have been turned away
by the salesman's stomach,
so heavy as he bent
to the drawer for his brochure,
he had to lean on the cabinet
with one small arm.
But when he stood up
and they saw how he had pushed
the stomach deep into his pants,
cinching the buckle high above it
as if to say, Here I am
above the belt, a normal man,
they were moved by his effort
to resemble them. The truth is,
sitting down at the table,
where the stomach disappeared,
he was like them, except
for his sorrow, which at first
they could not lift away.
Yet choosing the things they most
wanted from his brochure,
they soon brought a smile
to his face. Soon, at the door,
they were shaking his hand
like old friends, just before
they returned to their old hunger,
the anticipation of happiness
they carried like a weight.

THE WISH

Each time her mother
called her into the bedroom
and waved at her to shut
the door on her own father,
she knew it was because
the doctor was coming over, but
didn't care. All she wanted
was for the baldheaded woman
going farther and farther away
to return to the dim light.
She did not think how scary
it was to lock herself inside
the amber room with all
the shades pulled down or how,
propped on the amber pillow,
her mother looked like
a stuck fly. All she asked
was that her mother point down
at the bottom bureau drawer
so she could open it up
like always, saying, This?
turning back with the silk nightie
and This? showing the makeup
and the wig, meaning you and I
are talking now, stay right here.
For it was beautiful just
to have her mother raise
her arms so she could pull
the nightie up over the breasts,

shrunk now to the size of her own
breasts, and lovely to see the smile
as their breaths mingled
and her mother closed
her eyes. She did not think
as she applied the pinks
and reds about the wish
for love that was not possible,
so drawn by the love
that was, now handing her mother
the mirror so she could see
the happy woman in it saying,
Thank you, Thank you,
both of them smiling, neither
thinking of opening the door.

DISAVOWAL

Go ahead and believe
that this vacant house
in the shifting grass

remembers those nights
when the husband's headlights
flew against its side.

It is only a house.
How could it know the wife
stood each day at its window—

that thin wall
between her and everything
she wanted—or hear

the dutiful child
taking apart and putting
together the same, sad

cluster of notes. Go ahead
and think that in the darkness
under the eaves

it is aware
of this new couple
turning into the driveway

to approach its silent door:
the frowning man with the key,
the wife amazed by the view,

their daughter running across
the roof-shaped shadow
shifting in the wind.

THE MATCH

It is not clear why she ever
got into the ring in the first place,
ding-toed, all hips, swinging
like a girl. But it is she
who lands the first punch, right
on his proud chin. Nobody hits me there,
his whole body seems to say,
and he whirs his gloves
under her nose in such a way
she understands he is offering the chin
and pops him again. By the middle rounds
when the blood breaks out on his head
and it is certain he never intended
to hit her, she just stands
with her gloves down
waiting for him to come to her.
Who will stop the fight is the question
their children, having watched
from the front row for as long
as they can remember, never ask,
knowing it will only continue,
knowing there is no life outside the fight,
which they take with them
when they leave, on their way
into the lives of others. Alone at last
in the late rounds, the old boxers
clinch, embracing each other for the first
time in years. They are smiling,

he sure she can't hit him
as long as he holds her like this,
she knowing he is in her control forever
and ever, their kind of love.

THE MAP

When the wind
that has never stopped
blowing there is right,

I hear the voice
next door running down
on the gramophone. Over

and over she says lips
like wine and please
be mine,

only to me
lying in the dark.
Behind her wall

the people
laugh and laugh,
and in the huge

map of the tree-
shadow moving
on my shade

I find no river
or road to tell
where my lost

father has gone.
I love you and promise
true, she says to me,

this boy left here
in the wind,
listening to her fall

fast asleep
with the needle
at her throat,

searching the immense,
impossible
map.

This little boy with the taped glasses,
the dreamy kid nobody would put in charge
of details—he is the one I must slip inside
to look up into the toothless, angry face
of my mother whose voice does not come
all the way out of her mouth. Have I forgotten
my lunch box at school? Is this the day
I lost my paper-route list? What I know
is that standing above me in her red bathrobe
and waving her switch, she is about to ask
if I will ever do it again until I cannot
say no. What I know, tasting salt afterward
in my bed, is that she never got
the brand-new teeth. Did I only dream
she kissed me, father gone, under the lamplight
and told me of the lovely white smile
that would change her life, my life—
or did it happen? Now I am looking up
to find her at the sewing machine again
with only sharp pins between her lips
and in her hands the bright needle moving oh
so quick and deep. Now all her work of shirtsleeves
and pantcuffs is cleared away, and I am singing.
Before me, in the lamplight, a shut-faced man
sits listening in dark lapels. There at his side,
my happy mother, wearing lipstick, cannot stop
smiling at me with somebody else's mouth.

THE LAST TRICK

What I remember most
was not the teeth
the man next door
could pop out
of his mouth and push
forward on his tongue,
or even the hula girl
moving under the hair
of his forearm,
but how afterward,
his shirt buttoned
at the wrist, he looked
like any other adult,
patting my head
and smiling.

BLAME

Now my mother has a new man
to sit with, only the back
of a head from my angle
in the rear seat, with curly hair
I've never seen in our family
before. Everything seems new,
even the rummage-sale shirts
my brothers and I are wearing, even
the old Ford he's spent so long
fixing and shining for this ride
on the superhighway. I'm
the one who notices the trace
of blue above us, beautiful at first
as it gathers into a wide, long
ribbon. Then it transforms
into a haze my older brother
calls smoke in a loud voice,
and we are all suddenly opening
the doors and standing outside
the car in the breakdown lane.
Who is to blame for this misfortune
in my family's uncertain,
hopeful life? Not my mother,
so pleased seconds ago to have us
traveling together, not my brothers
and I, looking forward to our trip
into America's future, not
my stepfather, who, having no one

to accuse for the bad luck
he cannot change, goes around
and around the billowing car,
blaming each tire with his foot.

Raised during the Depression, my stepfather
responded to the economic opportunity
of the 1950s by buying more
and more cheap, secondhand things
meant to transform his life.
I got this for a hundred bucks,
he said, patting the tractor that listed
to one side, or the dump truck that started
with a roar and wouldn't dump.
Spreading their parts out on his tarp,
he'd make the strange whistle
he said he learned from the birds
for a whole morning
before the silence set in.
Who knows where he picked up
the complete A–Z encyclopedias
embossed in gold and published
in 1921? They were going to take these
to the dump, he said. Night after night
he sat up, determined to understand
everything under the sun
worth knowing, and falling asleep
over the book of A. Meanwhile, as the weeks,
then the months passed, the moon
went on rising over the junk machines
in the tall grass of the only
world my stepfather ever knew,
and nobody wrote to classify

his odd, beautiful whistle, formed,
somehow, in the back of his throat
when a new thing seemed just about to happen
and no words he could say expressed his hope.

WEEDS

In my fifty-fifth year,
kneeling in my garden
to pull a weed,
I discover my father,
whom I hardly knew,
lying down in his garden.
His heart so damaged now
no doctor would remove
the cataracts that spoil his sight,
he has no other way to see
what he is doing. With him again
in his sad dimness,
I don't want to lecture him
about the smell of booze,
or talk about the seed
he left long ago untended.
Aging father with my own
flaws of the heart,
I am content to see him
resting among the carrots
and peas. It is enough
to listen to him sip
the air in the innocence
of his concentration,
doing his best with the weeds.

Fine

FINE

Asked how he is, the sorrowful Russian
twists his hand one way to show how the thumb
depends on the fingers, another to show the fingers
depend on the thumb. In America we say Fine,
thank you, as if we had handled well-being
all by ourselves. Of course, we are lying.
As far back as grade school we learned the limits
of our production. Remember doing piece work
at the desks of that factory with Eddie Engel
and Karen Pinkham, turning out math problems
against the clock like so many chair legs or soles
of shoes? Fine, our teachers wrote
across our work with the Rhinehart method
but only on the days we didn't laugh
or talk or stare out the window at the blue sky.
Some classmates may still be there, kept after school
in the sad twilight, bewildered by a chair leg
they've made too short or too wide. The rest of us,
the ones they passed on to high school, grew pimples
and nether-hair and monstrous thoughts. Looking us over
our fathers concluded, You'll never make anything
of yourself. Our mothers said, You're not
going out of this house looking like that.
How could they have guessed we'd turn out fine,
showing up for the interview in a white shirt or blouse
nicer than our mothers ever dreamed. Who we are,
having learned at last the handshake and attitude
our elders wanted from the start, we're not
quite sure ourselves, but doesn't it all have to do

with the smiles on our interviewers' faces
as they take us to our desk in a room that might
make even the Russian feel things could be worse?
Outside the window the sky was never so fine.

FACES

It's not easy in America to look
into the mirror for the perfect face
as seen on TV and find yours instead,
sad-mouthed or bug-eyed or no hair
except the four or five sprouts coming in
at the end of your nose. So what's wrong,
you say, adjusting your collar
under the globes of light, with looking sincere
or interesting or distinguished? Meanwhile,
the face of the anchorman, handsome
in the confident way everyone's come to expect
from an American, tilts his hair
to enjoy the weather girl's little joke,
and the kind, sensible face of the expert
on diarrhea holds up a diagram
to warn you of your body's next eruption.
Wouldn't it be nice to be a face,
like the wholesome, smiling woman
who comes on next, relieved of both her body's
symptoms and her body? Not you, your body's
the very thing that brought the sorrow
to your lips and made your hair fall out
in the first place. Here you are arriving
at your shit job so gorged with blood
and out of breath, you can't apologize
for being late. Here you are
at the affair's end walking the dim halls
of the subway. Around you pictures of faces
advising aspirin or a cheap holiday

in the islands have missing teeth
and dicks in their mouths. Nobody likes them,
who have nothing to do with our lives
in America, the ones that you
and everybody else most want to be.

Two weeks after the saleswoman told the farm brothers
to wear condoms so she wouldn't get pregnant,
they sit on the porch wondering if it's all right
to take them off. They are about as bewildered
as the man at the bar whose head is tiny
because he asked the fairy godmother, granter of all
wishes, for a little head. Except for a moment,
you get the feeling, none of them have been that happy
about being attached to the preposterous requirements
of the things between their legs, which, in their resting
state, even the elephant thinks are a scream.
"How do you breathe through that thing?" he asks
the naked man. What the naked man replies, looking down
with this new view of himself, the joke doesn't say,
though he's probably not about to laugh. On the other
hand, what was so funny about our own stories
as boys and girls when we heard our first ones,
suddenly wearing patches of hair that had nothing
to do with Sunday school or math class? How lovely
that just as we were discovering the new distance
between ourselves and polite society, the secret
lives of farm girls and priests were pressed
into our ears. Later, when we found ourselves
underneath house mortgages and kids' dental bills,
having taken up the cause of ideal love, they got funny
because they'd never heard of it, still worried,
say, about penis size, like the guy who had his
lengthened by the addition of a baby elephant's
trunk and was doing fine until the cocktail party

where the hostess passed out peanuts.
Their obsessions revealed at the end of their jokes,
they have always been losers, going back to Richard Nixon,
who tried oral sex but never could get it
down Pat, going all the way back to Eve,
thrown out of the Garden for making the first candy,
Adam's peanut brittle. Yet let us celebrate the characters
of dirty jokes, so like us who have made them
in the pure persistence of their desire,
the innocent wish to find a way out of their bodies.

LOSSES

It must be difficult for God
listening to our voices come up
through his floor of cloud to tell Him what's
been taken away: Lord, I've lost my dog,
my period, my hair, all my money.
What can He say, given we are so incomplete
we can't stop being surprised by our condition,
and He is completeness itself? Or is God
more like us, made in His image—
shaking His head because He can't
be expected to keep track of which
voice goes with what name and address, He being
just one God. Either way, we seem to be left
here to discover our losses, everything
from car keys to larger items we can't
search our pockets for, while those around us,
like the compassionate expert on overweight
holding the hand of the hugely obese
woman on TV, offer their best advice.
She is crying because she's just learned
it isn't really self-control she's lost,
but only her self-esteem, which she can gain back
with a few simple steps. It's not difficult
to picture her after the applause
and the last commercial returning to sadness
and a jumbo bag of chips. The hard thing
about loss is, you've got to face it on your own.
Even though they give you music
to listen to and the dental assistant looks down

with her lovely smile, it's still your tooth
the dentist yanks out, leaving a soft
emptiness you'll ponder with your tongue
for days. Left to ourselves, we always go over
and over what's missing—tooth, dog, money,
self-control, and even losses as troubling
as the absence the widower can't stop
reaching for on the other side of his bed
a year later. Then one odd afternoon,
watching some ordinary happening like the way
light from the window holds a vase
on the table, or how the leaves
on his backyard tree change colors all at once
in a quick wind, he begins to feel a lightness,
as if all his loss has led to finding
just this. Only God knows where
the feeling came from, or maybe God's
not some knower off on a cloud, but there
in the eye, which tears up now at the strangest
moments, over the smallest things.

Love Handles

"Give it time," we say knowingly, as if time
were the preferred brand of motor oil
or a vitamin drink that makes the children grow
up right, though considering how time
can sometimes deal us a car that blows its engine
no matter what oil we use, or a vitamin-fed child
who grows into a ghoul, we haven't said enough. Time's
not ours to give, for one thing, nor is it, as in "It
will happen in its own good time," always good.
Take the aging bank president, for instance,
who in just five years has become the meek one
of the two, sitting beside his wife in church
as though she were his mother, and whispering
all through the service to nobody, not even
himself. Time, of course, couldn't care less,
which is why, seeing him or the lady with the cane
and pills who spends the whole day drinking nothing
so she won't have to get up and pee, we say, "If I
ever get like that, take me out and shoot me,"
our way of holding firm against the fact
that our own days are limited and Time
has all the time in the world. There are so many
ways to resist our uncertain, short futures,
like stopping off in a favorite decade,
as the late-60s couple has done, she
with the long dress, he with the whitening
ponytail. Or, if we want to play for keeps,
we could leave this time-cursed world by going
into the arms of Christ and never coming out,

or vanishing forever into work like the happy
bureaucrat spanking his hands after each task completed
"in a timely manner." But since Time will go on
dusting our hair, and creasing our hands
whatever we may do with them, perhaps
the best way is to put aside our fear of change
and death (fear being the only death we'll ever know
in life) and forget the wishful thought
that time makes good things happen to us,
thinking instead of time as the one medium we have
to make ourselves happen. Not through some step-
by-step program that helps us free the inner child
or get irresistible breasts in just seven days,
but slower and less organized, like the process
of sorrow that might begin in the heart
of the bureaucrat at the height of his pleasure
in finishing his job, or the unexpected flicker
of relief the bank president's wife,
meek all her life, might start to feel
as she stands up beside her spent husband in church
to sing. The hymn's words are about living forever
out of Time, though suddenly all she can think about
is living in it, as she has never quite done. Never mind
the regret and guilt she'll have to endure now,
she can't live without it, any more than the bureaucrat
or you or I can live without whatever pain might come
from recognizing that time has no truer measure
than our own heartbeat. Who says, anyway,
that the span of human life amounts to nothing
but a speck in time? The truth is, it's *our* speck.

SHAKING HANDS

Women, who have a choice, mostly
avoid it. They know it's a guy
thing anyway, so meeting in couples,
they let the men bend and put
their hands out as if to say
with their bodies go ahead and touch me,
but only there. Our fathers,
who wouldn't be caught dead
holding the hand of a man
on any other occasion, taught us how,
not the fish handshake, but a firm grip,
the idea being to reach out to someone
in such a way as to prove you don't
need to, adding it's good to meet you,
which means I'm a winner as you can see
from how I'm trying to rip your arm off.
OK, maybe they were trying to protect us
from the world's takers, the hand-
pumping car salesman, the politician,
the minister whose slow, soulful
rotation makes you want to hang on
to your wallet. But what if in this world
of pain and hardship you find a person
who can only offer the fish, like the man
I once shook with, discovering just
as I looked into his serious eyes
to say how good it was, I was squeezing
a hand that was nothing but a long thumb,
seeing only then all he was asking

me to understand as I met him.
What if nobody is a winner
and, meeting among our losses,
the wisest among us shake hands
aware of how little we have to assert.
The neighbor's husband, coming shyly
out of the TV room adjusting his pants
while she announces who he is,
would make our fathers just shake
their heads. Look at the smiling
dread with which he extends his hand,
less a real man than a lover who can't
imagine you'll take it. Take it.
He is the one your father would
have been if he were less afraid
to be afraid, the one who will allow
you, in this small event of reaching out,
to start again, making a good impression
by accepting just who he is,
and who, behind the face you've learned
for shaking hands, inside your hand, you are.

O feet, when they called me "Beanstalk"
at 14, meaning my body was what suddenly happened
after the planting of magic beans, my arms
startled branches, my head looking down from the sky,
I scarcely heard, stunned as I was by what magic
had done overnight to you. Bad enough I now owned a penis
so unpredictable I had to put books
on it walking down school halls, I had your long
arches and toes which, whatever I put on them, stuck out
all the more. Great pedicles, those first cordovans
were the worst, deep maroon dream shoes
that floated footless on their page in the catalogue
I ordered from, and arrived dead weights
in a huge box, so red and shiny
and durable, their names lasted through two years
of high school: Clodhoppers, Platters, Skis.
And years later, when I took you to dinner parties
where they were too polite to name you
and just stopped talking altogether—when I sat
with legs crossed holding my teacup in that parlor
in Chile and suddenly noticed the small people
seated around me were staring at how the pulse
lifted my big foot as it hung there in front of them,
was I any better off? How could I tell them
that I understood they had all they could do
not to begin crossing themselves right there,
that inside my foot and my outsized body,
I only wanted to be small, too? But peace,
old toe-lifters, if I couldn't accept you then,

if just last month I stood barefoot before my family
and called you in jest my Oscar Meyer five-packs
wiggling a big toe while singing, as in
the commercial, "I wish I were an Oscar Meyer wiener,"
forgive the bad joke and the accusations, this
has never been your fault. Unconcerned with fitting in,
all you ever wanted was to take me in the direction
of my own choosing. Never mind the hands
getting all the attention as they wave to others
on the street, this is not their poem,
but only yours, steady vessels, who all along
have resisted my desire to be like everyone else,
who turn after the hands are done and carry me
with resolute steps into my separate life.

CLOTHES

For days we are infatuated
with new clothes, giving our bodies
to them, wanting nothing more
than to be seen with them until the moment
we notice in the mirror they make our stomachs
stick out or our hips too big. Then they're back
behind a door in the dark with all the rest
whose only offense is failing to hide
who we are from others. We distrust them
from the moment somebody says how terrific
we look in them, relaxing only when they have spots
we can't get out or buttons missing,
so we can throw them in a chair when we're done
with them or right on the floor. Do we really hate
ourselves that much? the clothes might ask
but don't, being unable to speak, or maybe
since they're so close to us, just knowing
it's actually self-love that makes us feel good
to have nothing to do with hangers
or creating the correct impression,
like the clothes themselves, who have their best
time hanging out on the line, the dress shirts
swinging by their sleeves beside socks and underwear,
our new slacks with their pockets out,
kicking up their cuffs in the wind.

THE RETARDED CHILDREN PLAY BASEBALL

Never mind the coaches who try
to teach them the game,
and think of the pleasure

of the large-faced boy
on second who raises hand and glove
straight up making the precise

shape of a ball, even though
the ball's now over
the outfield. And think of the left

and right fielders going deeper
just to watch its roundness
materialize out of the sky

and drop at their feet. Both teams
are so in love with this moment
when the bat makes the ball jump

or fly that when it happens
everybody shouts, and the girl
with slanted eyes on first base

leaps off to let the batter by.
Forget the coaches shouting back
about the way the game is played

and consider the game
they're already playing, or playing
perhaps elsewhere on some other field,

like the shortstop, who stands transfixed
all through the action, staring
at what appears to be nothing.

BIG DOG, LITTLE DOG

Peeing, for instance,
is for him a lift-legged dangling
of string

down a fern
or snow hole; for her a kind
of sitting—one dainty hind

leg lifted up like a pinky
finger at teatime.
His wag clears china

off the sidetable; hers
doesn't exist,
only a boing. Boing

hello, boing
pick me up, boing
leave that front door open

and I'm off
to see the wizard. Big dog,
on the other hand, is off

his feet mostly. Day
after day she investigates
the huge what-was-him,

then sniffs her
empty bowl, the one sure
sign he is not dead,

but will rise again, his head
straining upward, his arthritic legs
scrambling to center it. Poor big

dog, anybody but she
would say. She'd rather
sniff the under-

parts as they
come up from the floor.
The two are, anyway,

close enough to sleep
together, which after he shlups
water and lies down to shlup

himself, they do. big dog
the undulance of fur
little dog drifts off

upon, leaving aloft
a miniature
periscope of ear.

WAVING GOODBYE

Why, when we say goodbye
at the end of an evening, do we deny
we are saying it at all, as in We'll
be seeing you or I'll call or Stop in,
somebody's always at home? Meanwhile, our friends,
telling us the same things, go on disappearing
beyond the porch light into the space
which except for a moment here or there
is always between us, no matter what we do.
Waving goodbye, of course, is what happens
when the space gets too large
for words—a gesture so innocent
and lonely, it could make a person weep
for days. Think of the hundreds of unknown
voyagers in the old, fluttering newsreel
patting and stroking the growing distance
between their nameless ship and the port
they are leaving, as if to promise I'll always
remember, and just as urgently, Always
remember me. Is it loneliness too
that makes the neighbor down the road lift
two fingers up from his steering wheel as he passes
day after day on his way to work in the hello
that turns into goodbye? What can our own raised
fingers do for him, locked in his masculine
purposes and speeding away inside the glass?
How can our waving wipe away the reflex
so deep in the woman next door to smile
and wave on her way into her house with the mail,

we'll never know if she is happy
or sad or lost? It can't. Yet in that moment
before she and all the others and we ourselves
turn back to our separate lives, how
extraordinary it is that we make this small flag
with our hands to show the closeness we wish for
in spite of what pulls us apart again
and again: the porch light snapping off,
the car picking its way down the road through the dark.

GLASS NIGHT

Come, warm rain
and cold snap,
come, car light

and country road
winding me around
dark's finger,

come, flash
of mailbox and sign,
and shine

of brush,
stubble and all
the lit lonely

windows wrapped
in the glass branches
of tree

after flying tree.
Come, moon-coated
snow hills, and flung

far ahead pole
by pole the long
glass cobweb

in my high beam
that carries me deeper.
Come, deeper

and mute dark
and speech of light.
Come, glass night.

Everyone else is in bed, it being, after all,
three in the morning, and you can hear
how quiet the house has become each time
you pause in the conversation you are having
with your close friend to take a bite
of your sandwich. Is it getting the wallpaper
around you in the kitchen up at last
that makes cucumbers and white bread, the only
things you could find to eat, taste so good,
or is it the satisfaction of having discovered
a project that could carry the two of you
into this moment made for nobody else?
Either way, you're here in the pleasure
of the tongue, which continues after
you've finished your sandwich, for now
you are savoring the talk alone—how
by staring at the band of fluorescent light
over the sink or the pattern you hadn't
noticed in the wallpaper, you can see
where the sentence you've started, line
by line, should go. Only love could lead you
to think this way, or to care so little
about how you speak, you end up saying
what you care most about exactly right,
each small allusion growing larger
in the light of your friend's eye.
And when the light itself grows larger,
it's not the next day coming through the windows

of that redone kitchen, but you,
changed by your hunger for the words
you listen to and speak, their taste
which you can never get enough of.

LOVE HANDLES

If the biker's head where the hair was
shines in the sun while he blows
into his helmet to get the heat out
of it, she doesn't mind. It's not him
with the bald spot, it's just him. And she likes
feeling the fleshy overhang in the front
when she climbs on behind and takes him
into her arms. How else could he carry her
up and up the wild, quick, five-
note scale that they float off on? Anyway,
who doesn't love a belly? Forget the revulsion
we're supposed to feel looking at the before picture
in the diet ad and remember the last time
you asked a good friend you hadn't seen in years,
What's *this?* patting where the shirt
stuck out. Or think of feeling somebody's
back, like the two old lovers lying in bed, she
turned away from him inquiring over her shoulder
with her finger, What's that, right there, is it
a bug bite or a mole? And he, the one trusted
with this place so private not even she
can see it, touching it, not skin or flesh
in this special, ordinary moment but something
else, something more, like the hand the hunched
old lady has in hers going across the fast-food
parking lot. Beside her an old man, the hand's
owner, is walking with what you and I
might think of as a sort of kick
over and over, but what they don't think of at all,

balancing each other like this so they can arrive
together to get a burger. The point is, you can't
begin to know how to hold another body
in your eye until you've held it a few times
in your hand or in your arms. Any ten couples
at the Fireman's Ball could tell you that. Put aside
your TV dreams of youth running its fingers
over the hood of a new car, or the smiling
faces of Tammy the weather girl and Bob on sports,
she with the unreal hair and he with the hair
that's not real, and imagine the baldies
with their corsaged wives under the whirling
chunks of light at the Ball. Think of their innocence,
all dressed up to be with the ones they've known
all their lives. See how after those years
of nudging and hugging and looking each other all over,
they glide, eyes closed, on love handles across the floor.

About the Author

The recipient of grants from the Rockefeller, Fulbright, and Guggenheim Foundations, Wesley McNair has held an NEH Fellowship in Literature and two NEA Fellowships for Creative Writers. He has won the Devins Award for poetry, the Eunice Tietjens Prize from *Poetry* magazine, the Theodore Roethke Prize from *Poetry Northwest,* the first prize in poetry from *Yankee* magazine, and the 1997 Sarah Josepha Hale Medal. He wrote the scripts for a series on Robert Frost that aired on PBS television and received a New England Emmy award. *Talking in the Dark* is his fifth volume of poetry, following (among others) *The Town of No* and *My Brother Running,* which were reissued in a single volume by Godine in 1997. Wesley McNair directs the creative writing program at the University of Maine at Farmington and lives with his wife, Diane, in Mercer, Maine.

Talking in the Dark

was set in Bembo, a design based on the types used by Venetian scholar-publisher Aldus Manutius in the printing of De Aetna, written by Pietro Bembo and published in 1495 by Francesco Griffo who, at Aldus's request, later cut the first italic types. Originally designed by the English Monotype Company, Bembo is now widely available and highly regarded. It remains one of the most elegant, readable, and widely used of all book faces.